Terry Fox

A Story of Hope

by **Maxine Trottier**

Scholastic Canada Ltd.
Toronto New York London Auckland Sydney
Mexico City New Delhi Hong Kong Buenos Aires

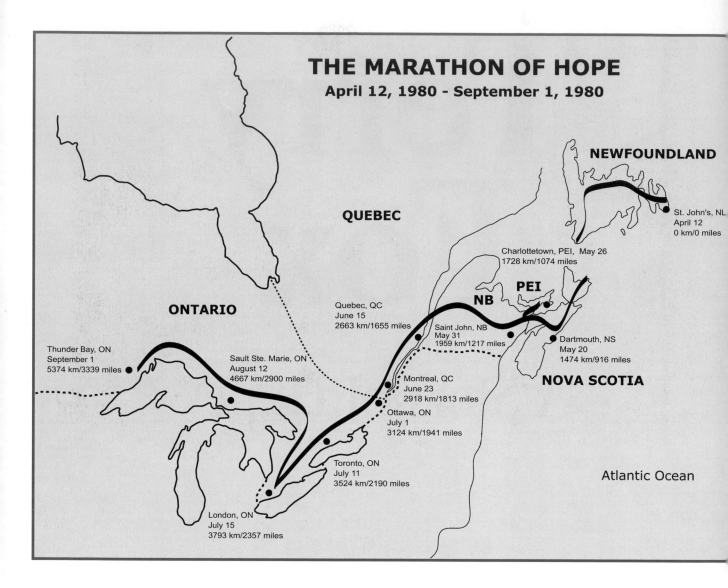

THE MARATHON OF HOPE
April 12, 1980 - September 1, 1980

NEWFOUNDLAND

QUEBEC

St. John's, NL
April 12
0 km/0 miles

Charlottetown, PEI, May 26
1728 km/1074 miles

ONTARIO

Quebec, QC
June 15
2663 km/1655 miles

NB

PEI

Saint John, NB
May 31
1959 km/1217 miles

Dartmouth, NS
May 20
1474 km/916 miles

Thunder Bay, ON
September 1
5374 km/3339 miles

Sault Ste. Marie, ON
August 12
4667 km/2900 miles

Montreal, QC
June 23
2918 km/1813 miles

NOVA SCOTIA

Ottawa, ON
July 1
3124 km/1941 miles

Toronto, ON
July 11
3524 km/2190 miles

Atlantic Ocean

London, ON
July 15
3793 km/2357 miles

Terry loved children. From his experiences with cancer, he knew they were far more courageous than he was, that they never gave up and always found a way to smile. This book is dedicated to those children who truly defined hope, and to the kids who cheered Terry on from St. John's, Newfoundland, to Thunder Bay, Ontario. It is dedicated to the children of those children who will read this story. Terry learned to dream big from kids just like you. Never doubt his words: "Anything is possible if you try. Dreams are made if people try."

— *Darrell Fox, August, 2005*

Hope is a quiet thing. It is about believing in a
dream, no matter how long and hard the road may
be. Hope is a young man running across Canada to
help find a cure for a disease that had caused so
much hurting. It is the echo of his footsteps
pounding on a lonely stretch of highway just
before dawn. Hope is the story of Terry Fox.

"Mom, I'm going to run across Canada."

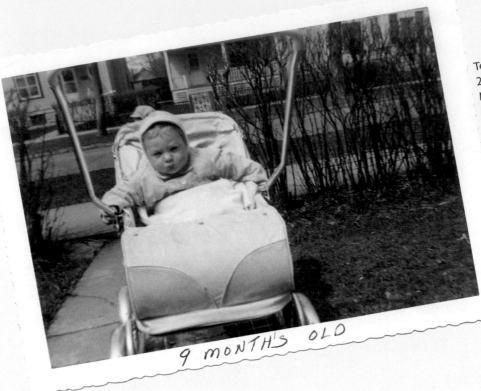

9 MONTH'S OLD

Terry Fox was born on July 28, 1958, in Winnipeg, Manitoba. This picture of him at 9 months was taken in front of the Fox home on Gertrude Avenue. Terry would grow into a determined boy, who even as a toddler showed the persistence with which he would face life's challenges.

It all began in a very ordinary way when Rolly and Betty Fox's son Terry was born. Patiently stacking and restacking his blocks, playing with toy soldiers — these things were a part of Terry's childhood. He built snowmen with his younger brother, Darrell, during the harsh Winnipeg winters and watched his baby sister, Judith, toddle around the house. There were family picnics and walks to school with his older brother, Fred.

Wearing their matching sweaters and pants made by their Grandma Wark, four-year-old Terry (right) and his brother Fred pose in front of the tree on Christmas morning.

Winnipeg, Man.
Novemeber 29, 1964
Dear Santa Claus,
    For Christmas I would like you to bring me a Battleground play set + a Johnny Seven gun.
    My little brother Darrell would like a train pull toy.
    Merry Christmas to you.
My address is 27 Camrose Bay
        Thank You
            Terry Fox

Even at the age of six, Terry's letter to Santa Claus, printed by his mom, shows that he thought not only of himself, but of his little brother.

A formal portrait of the smiling Fox family. Clockwise from left: 10-year-old Terry, Rolly, Fred (11 ½), Darrell (6), Judith (3), and Betty in the centre. Terry's mother worked as a homemaker; later on she would work part-time in a card shop. His father was a Canadian National Railway switchman.

Each year the Fox kids dressed up and had their portraits done by a photographer. Here, Terry is 10 years old.

Terry pitches to his mom at a local park. Fred is the catcher.

The Fox kids; Terry is on the right. By now the family lived in Port Coquitlam. The kids all loved to play for hours in the huge field behind their house on Morrill Street. Another favourite spot was the Coquitlam River. Terry walked to school and went home for lunch each day; he loved bread and jam.

Terry's grade eight Mary Hill school identification card from 1971-1972, the year that he became friends with a classmate named Doug Alward. The two shy, slightly built boys shared a love of biology and competitive sports.

In a pre-Christmas snapshot taken by Rolly in 1973, the rest of the Fox family stands in front of the fireplace in their living room. Terry is on the far right.

"I like challenges. I don't give up."

Then came a move to British Columbia. Port Coquitlam was the perfect place for the Fox kids to grow up. For Terry, there was roughhousing with his father and brothers and summer jobs picking blueberries, saving the money to buy his own clothes, a bike or school supplies. There were quiet times as well, when he would play alone for hours. School meant more than hard work; it meant new friends. One boy, Doug Alward, began a friendship with Terry that would endure for a lifetime.

Nine-year-old Terry, standing in the family's backyard, proudly holds a trophy won while playing baseball with his team, the Braves. Terry was a pitcher, catcher and first baseman.

Terry loved all sorts of sports. Here he is with his peewee soccer team, in 1971 in Port Coquitlam. Terry is third from the right, and Doug Alward stands next to him, behind the player with the ball.

And there were sports.

Terry played soccer, baseball and rugby. He competed in track and field and took up cross-country running, but what he wanted to do more than anything else was to play basketball. Terry was terrible at the game, yet he wouldn't give up his dream. All through the summer before grade nine, he played one-on-one with Doug. That fall, Terry ran to school each morning and stayed late after classes so that he could practise. The Fox stubbornness paid off. By grade ten, Terry had earned a place on the

By grade ten Terry was a starting guard on the Ravens, the Port Coquitlam Senior Secondary School basketball team. In this photo Terry is number 4, second from the left.

PORT COQUITLAM SECONDARY SCHOO

TERRY FOX

has been awarded this certificate for
meritorious accomplishment in

Scholarship

DATE   June 13, 1975

TEACHER

PRINCIPAL   John R Bowen

school basketball team, and when he and Doug graduated, they shared the Athlete of the Year Award. Terry enrolled at university and, more competitive than ever, he made the basketball team there. He had plans. Eventually he hoped to become a high school Phys Ed teacher. His future looked bright. Life was good.

"Mom and Dad didn't like me getting up early to go to school to play basketball...I'd run in the dark with all my books and clothes flying."

7

Terry's student ID from SFU.

The track and pool complex at Simon Fraser University, where Terry enrolled in the fall of 1976 to study kinesiology. Ever the athlete, he made the junior varsity basketball team there.

Judith, Terry and their mother at home, Christmas 1976. Terry and Judith are playing a game of "Operation."

Later, Terry relaxes in the front room with his sore leg extended.

Then, in November of 1976, Terry began having pain in his right knee. He tried to ignore it and continued to play basketball, but by March the pain was unbearable. His father drove him to the hospital where Terry had X-rays and a bone scan. With his family around him, he was told the results of the tests. He had bone cancer. His leg would have to be amputated as soon as possible. In an instant, Terry's life was changed forever.

At first, he cried at the thought of what had happened, at what faced him, but Terry pulled himself together. This was just one more challenge. He had worked hard before to achieve his goals and he could do it again, even if it meant doing it with only one leg. He wouldn't let anyone pity him, any more than he would pity himself.

Terry's fight with cancer had begun.

"Nobody is ever going to call me a quitter."

Terry was 18 years old when he was diagnosed with a type of cancer called osteogenic sarcoma and had his leg amputated. Within a month of his surgery, Terry was at home and walking using a temporary prosthesis with the help of crutches. He wouldn't need those crutches for long.

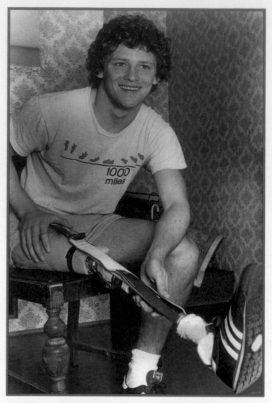

Terry's prosthesis with its straps and gears was made of steel and fibreglass. He would run two thirds of the way across Canada using this artificial leg.

Six days later, his leg was amputated and within a few incredible weeks he was learning to walk wearing a temporary prosthesis. He began chemotherapy at the cancer clinic. For Terry, those were difficult months. The suffering he saw there moved him deeply. When his treatment was finished, Terry left the hospital a changed person. He believed that he now had a debt to pay, that he would live his life to give courage to people who had been stricken by cancer. On the night before his surgery, he had read about an amputee runner,

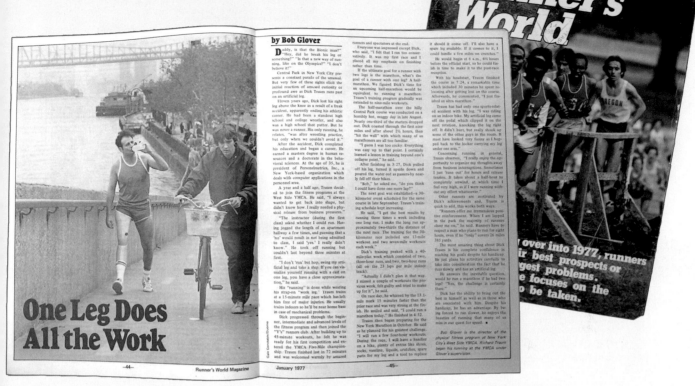

The *Runner's World* article in which Terry read about Dick Traum, a one-legged runner in the New York City Marathon. "I was lying in bed looking at this magazine, thinking if he can do it, I can do it, too."

a man who had run the New York City Marathon. It had filled him not only with admiration, but with hope. He now had a new dream, one that for the time being he kept to himself.

Terry Fox had decided that someday he would run across Canada to raise money for cancer research.

"That's the thing about cancer. I'm not the only one. It happens all the time to people."

Terry endured 16 months of chemotherapy. His hair fell out and he often felt weak and nauseated. During this time Rick Hansen asked him to play wheelchair basketball, and he eagerly rose to the challenge. In this image taken from a home movie, Terry shoots a basket in the SFU gym.

Terry receives the 1978 Canadian championship trophy for wheelchair basketball on behalf of his team, the Vancouver Cablecars.

On August 30, 1979, Terry headed to northern B.C. with Doug, Darrell and some friends to compete in the Prince George to Boston Marathon, a 17-mile race. He finished with a time of three hours and nine minutes, only ten minutes behind the last two-legged runner.

He began to train. Playing wheelchair basketball strengthened his upper body as well as his spirit. Running came next. Pushing himself a little farther each time, he built up his endurance and increased his strength. The day that he ran an entire mile was an enormous triumph for him. A double step with his left leg and a stride with his artificial leg. Over and over and over again. The prosthesis rubbed his stump raw and bloody, his bones were bruised, his foot blistered badly and he lost toenails, but he wouldn't give up. When Terry ran his first and only long-distance race, although he finished last, he finished. It was the biggest day of his life. Now he knew he could run across Canada.

"I broke it down. Get that mile down, get to that sign, get past the corner and around that bend... That's all I thought about."

Terry began writing heartfelt letters asking for support. He trained harder than ever, toughening himself for what was to come, ignoring the pain, making his plans, never losing sight of his dream. For months he continued to run around tracks, along roads, up and down hills, covering more than 3000 miles altogether. Finally he was ready.

Part of Terry's first letter, written with the help of his friend Rika Noda. Betty Fox helped Terry send other letters as well, to the Ford Motor Company, Imperial Oil, Adidas and other companies. They agreed to provide a van, fuel, shoes, food vouchers and money for the run. Although Terry appreciated the support, he steadfastly refused to endorse any business. He even insisted on wearing only clothing without logos.

I was rudely awakened by the feelings that surrounded and coursed through the cancer clinic....I could not leave knowing these faces and feelings would still exist. Somewhere the hurting must stop...and I was determined to take myself to the limit for this cause.

I feel strong not only physically, but more important, emotionally. Soon I will be adding one full mile a week, and coupled with weight training I have been doing, by next April I will be ready to achieve something that for me was once only a distant dream reserved for the world of miracles - to run across Canada to raise money for the fight against cancer.

The running I can do, even if I have to crawl every last mile. We need your help. The people in cancer clinics all over the world need people who believe in miracles.

Terry Fox, October 1979

14

"Somewhere the hurting must stop... I was determined to take myself to the limit for this cause."

While Terry ran, he counted telephone poles to help himself forget the pain in his foot and stump. He calculated his runs in miles; metric measurement had just become official in Canada in 1977. With one mile equaling 1.6 kilometres, Terry ran a total of 5084 kilometres during his training.

On the morning of April 12, 1980, Terry brought two empty glass jugs to Newfoundland's shore to fill with Atlantic sea water. One jug he planned to pour into the Pacific Ocean at the end of the marathon, the other he would keep as a souvenir. But the waves washed away one of the jugs. The one that he did fill sits in his parents' home today. With Doug Alward and a small crowd watching, Terry bent down to touch the stones and then dipped his leg in the harbour at the foot of Temperance Street in St. John's. He climbed the steep, gravelled hill to the road. The Marathon of Hope had begun.

If you had been in St. John's, Newfoundland, on that cold and windy day in April of 1980, you would have seen a young man dip his artificial leg into the Atlantic Ocean. You would have seen Terry Fox set out. You would have witnessed the beginning of an amazing journey: the Marathon of Hope.

Terry's postcard sent home to his mom, dad and Judith, postmarked Moncton, NB, May 30, 1980. It reads: "Hello, hope you are fine. Well I have made it to Charlottetown, P.E.I. Most beautiful country so far. People greeted me and followed me in from ten miles out of the city. Newfoundland's up to $40,000 now! Terry"

"I'm trying to raise as much money as I can."

Terry's friend Doug drove the van that had been donated for the run. In it was their gear, food and running shoes, three spare legs and some parts for repairs. Day after day, no matter what the weather, no matter how he felt, Terry ran. One mile at a time, with Doug waiting in the van up ahead, Terry pushed himself through Newfoundland and Nova Scotia. It wasn't easy, but each step was bringing him closer to the west coast of Canada, closer to home, closer to beating cancer. On he ran, from dawn until dusk, through Prince Edward Island and then New Brunswick, where his brother Darrell joined them. Into Quebec and then on to Ontario. The miles and the donations increased.

Terry's postcard home to Judith and his parents, postmarked Fredericton, NB, June 4, 1980. In it he talks about the "bucket," the fibreglass sleeve in which his stump sat:
"Hello! Hope you are fine. Great to have Darrell here. I'm having a tough week. Bucket isn't fitting right. Pain! 15 miles short of Fredericton now. Hope to get it fixed here. Terry"

Doug drives the van behind Terry as he runs. Until they reached Ontario and Terry was assigned a police escort, it was Doug and Darrell, 17, who looked out for Terry's safety on the road. Each day was tough. Enormous meals of pancakes, hamburgers, fries, beans and rice gave Terry energy and fuelled his body. The money he was raising fuelled his spirit.

"Some days it was so hard to get going; sometimes it was all pain."

Terry ran into Montreal, Quebec, wearing the French version of his Marathon of Hope T-shirt.

Terry ran an average of 26 miles a day, the equivalent of a marathon, for 143 days. With Doug driving the van, Darrell would gamely zigzag through traffic taking donations from passing motorists.

Terry runs along University Avenue in Toronto. He tried to acknowledge the thousands of people who came out to see him with a lift of his hand, what Darrell called a "Terry wave."

Terry didn't just run. During his months on the road he gave dozens of speeches, made endless phone calls, attended receptions and gave interviews. It was exhausting, but it did help raise money. At Toronto's Nathan Phillips Square, Maple Leafs captain Darryl Sittler presented Terry with his 1980 NHL All-Star team sweater. On that day Terry raised 100,000 dollars. He ran on, through the muggy summer weather, south to London and then back north. On July 28, Terry ran into Gravenhurst where he was welcomed with a 22nd birthday celebration.

So did the enthusiasm and warmth of Canadians everywhere. People cheered, urging Terry on with banners and signs. Some wept when they saw him pass by, his face a mask of concentration, while others stood in silence, touched by his courage and his cause. The eyes of the country were on a young man whose every step said that cancer could be beaten, that there was hope. He didn't care about being famous. He wasn't keeping a penny of the money being raised. One dollar was all he asked from each Canadian. One dollar. Terry Fox was running all the way across Canada, and he was going to make it. He had never been happier.

"If you've given a dollar, you are part of the Marathon of Hope."

On August 27, Terry had a rare opportunity to relax. Here he has just been swimming with a fellow amputee, 10-year-old Greg Scott, in Jackfish Lake, not far from Thunder Bay.

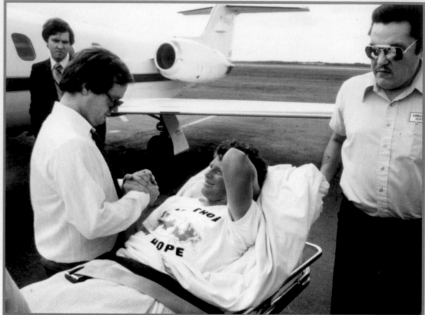

On September 2, Terry lies strapped on a stretcher waiting to be lifted into the small jet that would fly him, along with his parents, home to British Columbia for more treatment. He is talking to Bill Vigars, who worked for the Ontario division of the Cancer Society. Vigars had travelled with Terry and scheduled his appearances in Ontario. Like everyone else, he was stunned by the return of Terry's cancer.

But just outside of Thunder Bay, Ontario, the coughing and chest pain began. Terry asked Doug to drive him to a hospital. Before any tests were done, Terry was certain of what they would show.

He was right; the cancer had returned. Now it was in his lungs.

"...I began to think...there's something wrong. This may be the last mile."

Back in New Westminster, B.C. the same day, Terry, his mother and his father give a press conference at the Royal Columbian Hospital. In spite of the fact that Darryl Sittler, the Toronto Maple Leafs and the NHL offered to finish the run for him, Terry told the world he would do it himself someday.

With his parents at his side, Terry broke the news to the rest of Canada at a press conference. The nation was stunned. He had run 3,339 miles in just 143 days, and it all seemed so unfair. Terry, though, knew that cancer had nothing to do with fairness. He knew that what was happening to him could happen to anyone, and that now people would understand exactly what having cancer meant. Terry had done his best to run across Canada; he would do his best to fight this cancer and some day finish the run.

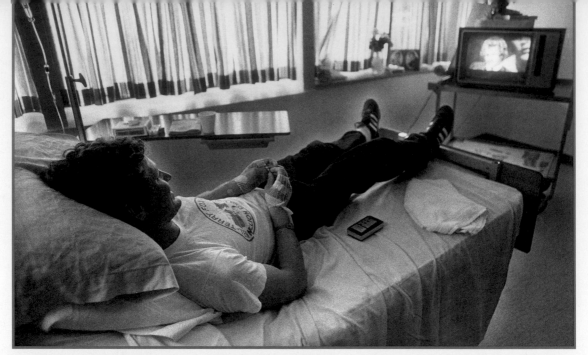

On September 7, 1980, Terry, who is undergoing more chemotherapy, lies in hospital wearing his Marathon of Hope T-shirt. He is watching a CTV fundraising broadcast that raised 10.5 million dollars for cancer research.

Buttons such as this one were a way that people demonstrated their involvement with Terry and the Marathon of Hope.

Young people were huge supporters of Terry during his run. They stuck by him and continued to raise money while he fought the return of cancer.

Terry met Isadore Sharp when he ran through Montreal. Sharp, a Montreal philanthropist whose teenaged son had died of cancer, was responsible for organizing a fundraiser among the businessmen in his city. Its motto was, "Let's Make Terry's Run Really Count." Later Sharp assured Terry that an annual run would be held in his name. Sharp still serves as a Director of the Terry Fox Foundation.

Terry's words shook our country. While he endured yet more chemotherapy, Canadians everywhere began to raise money. There was a telethon. There were walk-a-thons, run-a-thons, dances and recitals. Corporations donated huge sums, and children sold lemonade. By February, 1981, Terry's run and the generosity it had inspired had raised more than 24 million dollars, just as he had dreamed it would.

"We're really going to have to try hard in order to beat it, try harder than we ever have before."

Terry sits at home after attending a special ceremony on September 18, 1980, in which he became a Companion of the Order of Canada. He remains the youngest person to have received the honour. On October 21, he was awarded the Order of the Dogwood, B.C.'s highest civilian award. Since his death, schools across Canada, parks, an icebreaker and even a mountain in B.C. have been named after him.

Terry was showered with honours. Thousands of letters and telegrams of encouragement from Canada and all around the world poured into his hospital room and into the Foxes' home. People were still saying that they were behind him, that he shouldn't give up, that he could make it. Terry tried to beat the cancer. He fought harder than he had ever fought before, but some things are simply not meant to be, no matter how much we want them. Surrounded by his family, Terry died on June 28, 1981, just before dawn, the still and peaceful time when he most loved to run.

"Even if I don't finish, we need others to continue. It's got to keep going without me."

MR TERRY FOX
℅ ROYAL COLUMBIAN HOSPITAL
NEW WESTMINSTER
B.C.

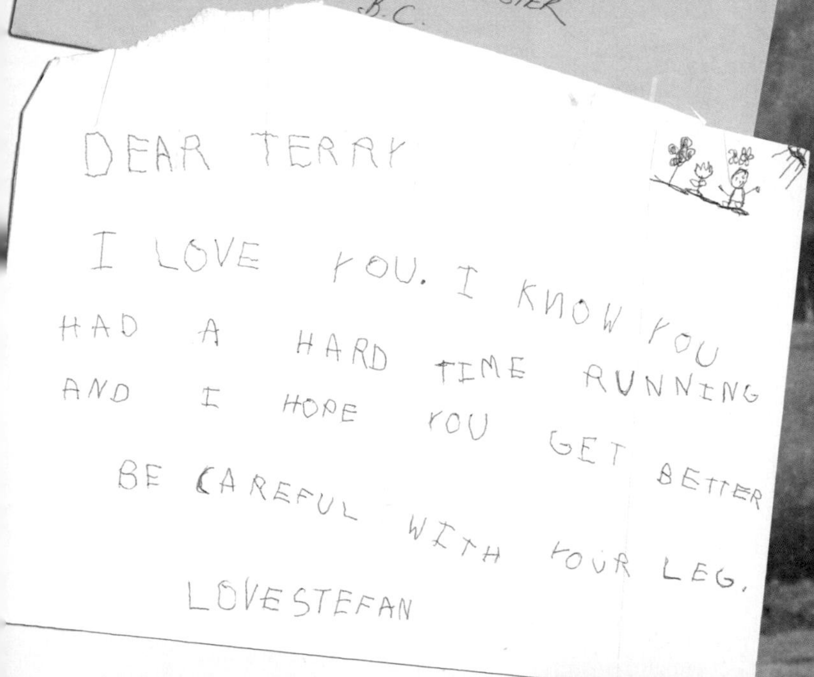

DEAR TERRY

I LOVE YOU. I KNOW YOU
HAD A HARD TIME RUNNING
AND I HOPE YOU GET BETTER

BE CAREFUL WITH YOUR LEG.

LOVE STEFAN

Terry's funeral on July 2, 1981, brought the country together in mourning. He was laid to rest in the Port Coquitlam Cemetery, not far from his favourite lookout, a quiet place where he sometimes went to think. Monuments honouring Terry can be seen in St. John's, Newfoundland, in Port Coquitlam and Vancouver, B.C., and in Ottawa. This one stands in Thunder Bay, Ontario.

Hope is a quiet thing, but if a dream is strong enough, hope can grow and grow until it touches everyone. Terry Fox's Marathon of Hope did not end on that morning. People are still running with his dream, people who believe in miracles, people who share Terry's certainty that anything is possible if you try. And because Terry Fox tried his best, because he ran his marathon and gave us his precious gift of hope, someday a cure for cancer will be found.

Someday the hurting will stop.

On April 4, 2005, the Royal Canadian Mint released a one-dollar coin with Terry's image on it, in honour of the 25th anniversary of his Marathon of Hope.

"Even though I'm not running anymore, we still have to try to find a cure for cancer. Other people should go ahead and try to do their own thing now."

Students parade down Main Street in Humboldt, Saskatchewan in September, 2004, to promote the annual Terry Fox Run.

Before Terry Fox died, he knew that an event would be held to continue his efforts to raise money for the fight against cancer. As Isadore Sharp had promised, the Terry Fox Run was established to carry on his Marathon of Hope. Held for the first time in 1981, it drew 300,000 participants across Canada, who walked, wheeled and ran to raise 3.5 million dollars for the cause. In Canada, the Terry Fox Run has been held each September since then, usually on the second Sunday after Labour Day. There is no entry fee and there are no prizes. Families, organizations, schools and individuals come together in a non-competitive event, with the help of thousands of volunteers, to keep Terry's dream of hope alive. Terry Fox Runs have spread throughout the world, to places like India and Ireland, and over 350 million dollars has been raised. The Terry Fox Foundation was established in 1988 as an independent non-profit organization to distribute the funds raised for cancer research in Terry's name.

You can find out more about the Terry Fox Run and the Terry Fox Foundation at www.terryfoxrun.org, or call toll free 1-888-836-9786.

Marathon of Hope memorabilia can be seen at the Terry Fox Library in Port Coquitlam and at the B.C. Sports Hall of Fame (Terry Fox Gallery) in Vancouver.

There are also several books about Terry:

Terry, by Douglas Coupland: a pictorial work with text for adults

Terry Fox: His Story, by Leslie Scrivener: a biography for adults

Run, by Eric Walters: a young adult novel

This book is for Carla Mota, Russ Lesperance and Marilyn McCormick. It is for Mike Pastorius and his remarkable family. It is for all people who have ever been touched by cancer.

My thanks to the Fox family for their generous input, and to my agent, Lynn Bennett, for her support. Thanks as well as to Andrea Casault, Diane Kerner, Heather Patterson, Solange Champagne-Cowle, and a small army of Scholastic staffers who made this book come together.

— Maxine Trottier

Scholastic Canada Ltd.
175 Hillmount Road, Markham, Ontario L6C 1Z7, Canada

Scholastic Inc.
557 Broadway, New York, NY 10012, USA

Scholastic Australia Pty Limited
PO Box 579, Gosford, NSW 2250, Australia

Scholastic New Zealand Limited
Private Bag 94407, Greenmount, Auckland, New Zealand

Scholastic Ltd.
Villiers House, Clarendon Avenue, Leamington Spa, Warwickshire CV32 5PR, UK

Library and Archives Canada Cataloguing in Publication

Trottier, Maxine

Terry Fox : a story of hope / Maxine Trottier.
ISBN 0-439-94888-6

1. Fox, Terry, 1958-1981--Juvenile literature.
2. Cancer--Patients--Biography--Juvenile literature.
3. Runners (Sports)--Canada--Biography--Juvenile literature. I. Title.

RC265.6.F68T76 2005   j362.196'994'0092
C2005-902058-X

Every effort has been made to trace ownership of visual and written material used in this book. Errors and omissions will be corrected in subsequent printings.

All photos and other materials are from the archives of the Fox family or the Terry Fox Foundation, except:
Borough of Scarborough: 1
Simon Fraser University: 8 (top left)
Courtesy *The Vancouver Sun* 10 (right)
Gail Harvey: cover, 19 (top left and lower left), 27
Marnie North: 20
Bill Becker/Canadian Press: 21
Andy Clark/Canadian Press: 24 (top)
Jeff Bassett/Canadian Press: 28 (top)
Courtesy Boris Spremo/*Toronto Star*: 22 (left)
Courtesy David Cooper/*Toronto Star*: 22 (right)
Courtesy Erin Combs/*Toronto Star*: 24 (lower left)
Courtesy *The Province*: 23
© Canadian Museum of Civilization, collection no. 981.10.115, photo Richard Taylor, S94-5512: 24 (button)
Coin image on page 28 © courtesy of the Royal Canadian Mint
Rob Muench, Humboldt, SK: 29
Canadian Press: back cover

7 6 5 4 3 2   Printed in Canada   05 06 07 08